P9-AQT-122

Building
Highly Effective Teams

How to Transform Virtual Teams to Cohesive
Professional Networks - A Practical Guide

Building
Highly Effective Teams

How to Transform Virtual Teams To Cohesive
Professional Networks - A Practical Guide

Michael Nir

Sapir Publishing, Boston, MA

658.3
ᴨᴜᴥ
2016

Third Edition © 2016 by Michael Nir

All rights reserved. No part of this publication may be reproduced, stored in a retrieval system, or transmitted in any form or by any means, electronic, mechanical, photocopying, recording, scanning, or otherwise except as permitted under Sections 107 or 108 of the 1976 United States Copyright Act without the prior written permission of the author.

This publication was designed to provide accurate and authoritative information about the subject matter covered. It is sold with the understanding that neither the publisher nor the author is engaged in rendering legal, accounting, or other professional services.

If legal advice or other expert assistance is required, the services of a competent professional person should be sought. Neither the publisher nor the author shall be liable for damages directly or indirectly arising herefrom.

ISBN 978-1492274940

ATTENTION CORPORATIONS, UNIVERSITIES, COLLEGES AND PROFFESIONAL ORGANIZATIONS!

Quantity discounts are available on bulk purchases of this book and the book can be completely customized for your organization to fit specific needs.

Contact us at **sapir@sapir-cs.com**

3 1712 01594 4542

Accolades for Building Highly Effective Teams

"Highly effective teaming seems so difficult to most of us, but as Nir demonstrates it is not. **Communication, honesty, integrity and effort make so much of the difference.** *This book is* **written clearly and moves rapidly through the material** *and goes into sufficient detail for implementation. Just like that!"*

"If I can read 50 pages and not 350 pages and get the same ... it's better having... read too many books that are longer and not to the point **I constantly look for these guide that provide with all I need in a practical manner.**"

"I find a case study provided in this guide to be very useful...case studies make or break business books and in this case **the case study provides what you need to know for building highly effective teams.**"

"Guide that focuses on the benefits of building highly effective teams as well as the main process steps of creating the teams – **relevant to managers and leaders in global organizations** *I guess – maybe also in smaller one."*

"The book contains **many relevant and important ideas for building highly effective teams,** overall general view with the use of a case study for explaining the concepts."

"This guide **delivers applicable tools and techniques for building high performance teams** in global and also virtual environments. The case study example provides necessary explanations to carry out the recommendations."

"Applicable tools and techniques presented with a case study **provide a powerful context for building high performance teams effectively in a global setting** which most of our businesses currently employ."

Preface

Congratulations! Thank you for purchasing this book and striving to learn practical methods to build a highly effective team.

Are you are at a loss when it comes to handling a virtual team? Have you read books and undertaken training to improve your virtual team's performance, but to no avail? Do you work in the virtual environment with people from all over the world?

Managing the virtual team is difficult and challenging, but this guide will uncover the secrets of building a high performing virtual team. After reading this guide, you'll know what to do to successfully and continuously manage your virtual teams.

This book is based on tested experience and hands-on interaction with global teams—leading programs and projects worldwide. It includes the practical essentials of how to build and lead highly effective teams globally. This book also forms the basis of a two-day high performance team workshop in which groups learn to operate as a cohesive integrated team and undergo a lasting transformation.

Join me in this journey to transform your (virtual) team's performance.

And, of course, everything in this breakthrough guide is relevant to collocated teams as well.

Preface to the 3rd Edition

I have reread this book often, adding concepts, editing, and restructuring. I also reviewed feedback from my readers and from participants in workshops I have led. This guide provides the essence of what makes a team high performing; nine must-haves are presented in the first chapter. It also discusses leader behaviors and presents two case studies showing how leaders can build high performance teams.

It has been a year since this book was originally released and it became a best-seller with over 100,000 copies sold. The time has come to release a new edition.

I contemplated for some time, "what can be the trump to add to this book?" and then I had the answer. In this third edition, I will share the step-by-step process of a two-day workshop that will turn your team into a high performance one.

This is top-rated content, which is rarely shared. I am transcribing my trainer notes into a process description. Read it and you will have a powerful tool to lead your team on the high performance journey.

Enjoy,
Michael,
Boston, 2016

Reader Tools

To enhance your reading experience, we use the following interactive tools in this book.

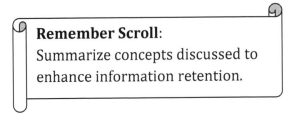

Remember Scroll:
Summarize concepts discussed to enhance information retention.

Case Study Paragraphs: *Mark stories that bring to life the issues discussed in the book.*

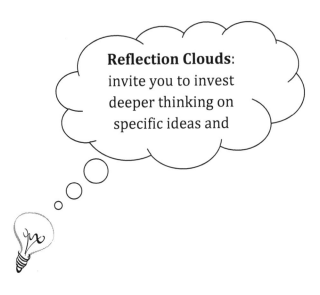

Reflection Clouds:
invite you to invest deeper thinking on specific ideas and

Contents

Leadership Behaviors in a Highly Effective Team 69

Introduction

For any virtual team to be effective, it must evolve into a high performance team. I say evolve because no team automatically starts out as a high performance team. You can take the most qualified experts, all of whom are excellent team players, and put them in a team together, but that doesn't make them a high performance team. They must learn how to work together to form a high performance team.

Any team has the potential to become a high performance team. This ability isn't so much dependent upon the expertise and ability of the individual members, although that does add to the team's performance, but rather, it depends on the commitment that each individual has to the team. As with many other things, we find in the business world that attitude counts for as much as ability.

We work together in teams to develop synergy. This elusive word refers to the increase in ability that happens when different elements work together. The ultimate result is greater than the sum of its parts. High performance teams capitalize on this, finding the way to achieve the greatest possible synergy in all their actions.

While the team leader is a critical part of this forming process, it doesn't all depend upon the team leader. The types of people who are chosen for the team, their individual abilities, their personalities, their communication skills, their levels of commitment, and their ability to work with others all affect this process. If not dealt with properly, a single person with the wrong attitude can keep the team from becoming high performance.

The
Must-Haves of
Highly Effective Teams

Before we go any further, we need to make sure that we're speaking the same language. We need to know what a high performance team is so that we also know what it isn't.

As with any team, high performance teams bring together a group of cross-disciplinary people to work together toward a common goal. Each member of the team brings specific skills, talents, and knowledge to contribute toward that goal. But that alone doesn't make the team high performance.

The team needs to meld together to the point where each team member is drawing on the skills and talents of the other team members. This comes about through building relationships, communication, and trust.

No team can become high performance without the commitment of its members. Not just a commitment to the team, but also a commitment to the team's success. There is an old saying that a chain is only as strong as its weakest link. In the case of a team, that weakest link is the team member who has the least commitment to team success.

When a team becomes high performance, it is demonstrated by high levels of collaboration and innovation, which helps the team produce superior results on a consistent basis. This isn't to say that the team never fails at anything, but to say that the team will work its way through those failures together, often by finding innovative ways of overcoming them and turning those failures into successes.

Certain actions are common in the development and behavior of a high performance team, which we can use to characterize these teams. This includes the nine must-haves of high performance teams.

Must-have #1: Develop clear goals and plans

Must-have #2: Effective communication

Must-have #3: Improve and maintain positive relationships among members

Must-have #4: Clarify roles and responsibilities

Must-have #5: Enhance mutual trust

Must-have #6: Solve problems and make effective decisions

Must-have #7: Value and promote diversity

Must-have #8: Successfully manage conflict

Must-have #9: Provide development opportunities and recognition

In the following pages are detailed descriptions of these nine must-haves.

Must-Have #1:
Develop Clear Goals and Plans

For any team to be effective, the team members need to know where they are going and how they are going to get there. Goals and plans aren't merely dictated to the team from above, but developed by the team as a whole, including intermediate goals used as milestones.

While all plans experience challenges that necessitate changes, without a plan, there is no way of knowing whether one is on track. However, it's not enough that the team develop clear goals; for the team to be high performance, every team member must buy into those goals as well.

"Buy-in" is comprised of presenting yourself to the greater good of the team's success. It has to be preached from the top-down and the behavior has to be modeled from top-down. I have learned during my coaching practice that "buy-in" must be communicated in many forms, from motivational handouts to public praise for desired behavior.

It is important that such communication occurs when appropriate. "Buy-in" always occurs when the leader empowers the team members to create a culture in which the members are a part of the process. In this context, "buy-in" is more than inspirational quotes; instead, it is a mentality and a belief, and it is the core and fabric that allows great things to happen collectively. Through the process of buying in, the team owns the goals and plans that they develop.

I have often witnessed newly appointed executives assembling their teams and presenting a flashy presentation in the boardroom to dictate the goals of the team. This approach usually fails; what's more, it creates a rift in the executive management team because without a proper "buy-in" process, they will not follow through on the goals.

In the modern matrix organization, this is also true for nearly all cross-functional teams: **without proper "buy-in," the goals are not shared.**

Point Blank – Take One

I started my career as an industrial engineer. I worked at a small consultancy, which collaborated with a bigger one. I was the junior consultant, halfway through a M.Sc. degree, and had just started writing my thesis. I was loaned to the bigger consultancy for an infrastructure project.

We were four consultants developing the construction program plans of a huge semiconductor manufacturing plant. We had little contact with our office and interacted with one another constantly. The leader of our small outfit was a veteran project manager, who had participated in three similar projects in the past.

As the financing for the program was still underway, we spent over half a year in a small 9×9 feet cubicle, trying to look busy. For me, this was completely discouraging. We were passing the time, waiting for the go-ahead with little to do. It was then that I experienced what always seemed ludicrous to me: it is better to have more work to do than less work.

We wanted to climb the walls out of boredom, but because it was a small cubicle, there were no walls to climb. At one point, our team manager spent four weeks deciding on the color layout of the kickoff presentation.

What we lacked most was leadership from our team leader and the managers of the consultancy. There was nothing much to work on, no glue connecting us, and no significance behind our long wait. The lack of a goal that could motivate us and a forward plan that could unite us was detrimental to our small team's morale. We complained and bickered; we criticized each other and were generally unproductive for the small tasks we still had to complete. I left this team less than one year into the role, frustrated and hoping that my future experiences would turn out better.

Remember, people need goals to align themselves with and to give them a sense of direction

Must-Have #2:
Effective Communication

A team that doesn't communicate isn't a team at all, but rather a group of individuals who are each marching to the beat of their own drums. High performance teams develop clear consistent methods for communicating with one another, both on a formal and informal basis.

This communication is collaborative in nature and provides constant feedback to each team member. By providing constant feedback, each team member feels more secure about the team relationship.

What's more, team communication processes that function effectively can increase team motivation, foster trust and respect between members, greatly improve decision-making processes, and contribute substantially to the overall productivity and performance of the team.

Nonetheless, ineffective communication processes can decrease member motivation, lessen team commitment, increase team gossip, and lower productivity.

Effective communication processes, therefore, are vital to team performance. What makes a communication process effective? Regularity and consistency, transparency and focus, and a direct correlation to team goals.

Regular communication within and between teams helps members to maintain focus. This allows all members to remain current regarding team progress and it ensures that difficulties or setbacks are handled promptly and collaboratively.

Transparent communication processes provide all team members with the same information, where possible, to keep all members adequately informed. Transparent processes maximize the likelihood that team members will be aligned in their concept of where they are going and how they are going to get there.

Failing to adequately inform all team members equally can greatly compromise their ability to contribute equally to team processes and decision

making. Communication processes that are focused
and **related to team goals encourage team
members** to also remain goal focused and outcome
directed.

Point Blank – Take Two

*My next position was as a project manager in a
high-tech start-up in the telecom industry. This was the
apex of the dotcom bubble bust, and the situation was
no different in our company. Rumors were abundant
and we were waiting for the axe to fall.*

*At the time, I was writing business requirement
documents for our development and engineering
department. The other six engineers, who had been my
seniors, were performing various product-marketing
roles.*

*Most of our meetings ended in gossiping sessions
concerning our chances of survival. These were based
on rumors, half-truths, and an ill-perceived
understanding of various executive messages. It was
difficult to concentrate on objectives and deliverables,
let alone produce robust business requirements based
on a collaborative effort. What's more, the team*

leader—the VP of marketing—instead of focusing on the work to be accomplished, was joining us in the speculations.

Clearly, this was not the best example for encouraging effective and focused communication.

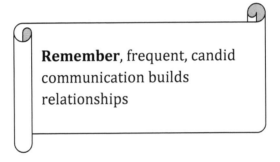

Remember, frequent, candid communication builds relationships

Must-Have #3:
Improve and Maintain Positive Relationships among Members

For team members to work together effectively, their relationships need to go beyond that of merely a business relationship. Members of high performance teams have social interaction outside the workplace to form bonds among individual members based on respect, trust, and knowledge of one another's capabilities.

Time must be taken to develop and maintain these relationships; this isn't wasted time, it is team-building time.

Building team relationships can be accomplished by encouraging team members to recognize each other's strengths.

For example, during morning briefings, let each team member identify some business trait they appreciate about the person seated to their left. Someone might recognize a co-worker's willingness to work late, while another team member might state that a teammate's organizational skills contribute to the group's efforts.

The process of recognizing each other's strengths is structured on empathy.

There is a great expression: **"People will forget what you said, people will forget what you did, but people will never forget how you made them feel."**

Empathy and understanding builds connections between people. It is a state of perceiving and relating to another person's feelings and needs without blaming, giving advice, or trying to fix the situation.

Empathy also means "reading" another person's inner state, interpreting it in a way that will help the other person, offering support, and developing mutual trust. The team leader promotes empathy by giving time to team members. Being present in the time you give to people is also important so that when you are with someone, you are truly with them and not dwelling in the past or worrying about the future.

The connections we make with other people are the cornerstone of our existence; devoting time, energy, and effort to developing and building relationships is one of the most valuable life skills.

Point Blank – Take Three

People tend to confuse empathy and sympathy. Empathy is the ability to understand other perspectives. **Sympathy** *is identifying with another's emotional state.* **Empathy** *is crucial for effective communication, sympathy for relationships with friends and family.*

The above expression reminds me of a training seminar I participated in a few years ago.

It was a full week Gestalt retreat where we held therapy learning sessions. Morning and afternoon small team meetings were led by a facilitator.

I remember one such meeting quite vividly when we were practicing self-disclosure as a way to increase empathy among team members.

Self-disclosure is sharing something personal to increase the empathy and contact between individuals; it is extremely powerful and leads to surprising results.

We were about halfway through the three-hour session when the facilitator thought I was holding back. She insisted I spend more time than the others on self-disclosure and she wouldn't let go.

I wasn't happy to be isolated, but I worked together with her accordingly. Whatever I felt supported to share was not enough, and when I mentioned it, she rebuked me rather nastily for not participating fully in the session.

I don't remember exactly what she said or did, but I remember I felt bad. This intense experience has been a great lesson and take-away.

I remember it vividly when leading sessions. I make sure to check how participants are feeling, and I make sure the team completes the interpersonal interactions prior to being dispersed.

Remember, "People will forget what you said, people will forget what you did, but people **will never forget how you made them feel**."

Must-Have #4:
Clarify Roles and Responsibilities

While the team is collaborating to accomplish goals, all of the team members must know they are part of the team because of their knowledge and experience.

Clearly defining the roles and responsibilities of each team member eliminates the problem of everyone thinking that someone else was completing a task, while nobody was really doing it.

Team goals and plans are broken down into individual areas of responsibility to ensure that each member knows how their area of responsibility helps the team accomplish the overall goal. Team members also know the roles and responsibilities of other team members, which facilitates effective collaboration.

Clearly identified roles and responsibilities also help to define where the team fits within the organization and who members report to, thereby

avoiding disputes and misunderstandings over
authority.

When defining roles and responsibilities in the
workplace, you might need to create a list of all of
your team members and a list of all tasks and roles in
the business.

You can then assign the roles to each staff
member or group. It is important to remain flexible
and be prepared to modify your plan in consultation
with your team.

Once you have defined each person's roles and
responsibilities, you can record this in a RACI matrix
chart. This can be as formal or informal as you prefer,
but it is important to record the key information.

RACI matrixes provide the opportunity to clearly
communicate each individual's roles and
responsibilities and they serve as a way to measure
performance by setting key performance indicators
(KPIs) against the tasks or requirements.

The RACI model is a powerful tool utilized to
define roles and responsibilities. In general, you

match up roles and responsibilities with processes.
RACI stands for

Responsible: The buck stops here. Whoever is
responsible must make sure that the process
operates as planned. The **R** owns the process,
problem, or project.

Accountable: This is the person who is
delegated the task of completing the activity. This
person supports the person who owns the **R**.

Consult: This person usually has in-depth
knowledge of the process in question and must
approve all major decisions.

Inform: The people in this group need to be
informed of activity taken, but not necessarily
consulted in decisions made.

**Failing to define workplace roles and
responsibilities can create tension,
miscommunication, and inefficiency in a business.**

People may be unsure as to their own jobs and
to whom they are required to report. Mistakes and

omissions can also occur when people are unsure of what is required of them, which can create inefficiencies that cost time and money.

Point Blank – Take Four

One of the assignments my company completed was project management at a petrochemical production plant. We managed the scheduling and budget control elements for a factory turnaround project. During this recurring project, the plant was shut down for approximately one month. During the execution, work is completed around the clock, 24 hours: equipment is refurbished, cleaned, fixed, etc.

The short but intense execution is completed subsequent to a year and a half of through engineering planning. The engineering design phase is not managed as a project, but the turnaround is. This leads to absurd situations during the hectic execution phase of the project. The responsible parties of the design planning are not explicitly identified and must be located when risks occur (unknown unknowns). At one time, because engineering was using outdated design documents, two pipes that had to meet were actually two feet apart.

Because the design team lacked proper accountabilities, it was challenging to find the proper solution quickly.

*Make sure you have **clearly defined responsibilities** and accountabilities.*

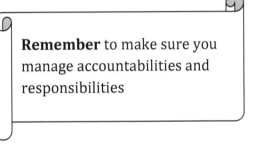

Remember to make sure you manage accountabilities and responsibilities

Must-Have #5:
Enhance Mutual Trust

Trust is one of the hardest qualities to develop in any team because it only develops through time and experience. Nevertheless, members of high performance teams must develop trust in each other and in the team as a whole.

Team members must see competence and commitment demonstrated by each other for this trust to grow. They must see that the other team members are committed to team success and not just personal success. They need to develop confidence both in the professional ability of other team members and their personal integrity.

All the must-haves previously described support the building of trust, but trust is a complicated aspect of relationships, and trust at the team level becomes even more complex. Trust increases communication, commitment, and loyalty among team members.

Trust can be considered a foundation that enables people to work together, and it is an

enabler for social interactions. It can also improve team performance and increase the probability of creating successful companies. Trust plays a crucial role when global business teams, start-ups, and networks are being created. In modern organizations, trust has become increasingly important because the organizations cannot rely on formal policies and rigid rules.

The team is a basic unit of performance for most organizations; it melds together the skills, experiences, and insights of several people. High-performing teams are not usually a collection of the brightest individuals. Rather, they are functioning entities that have diverse roles for the team members, who provide the skills and knowledge to succeed.

Healthy rivalry among team members enables the team to perform at a high level, but only if the team is built on robust trust. Trust building is a relatively slow process compared to other business processes, but it can be accelerated with open interaction and good communication skills. **Shared experiences create trust, and trust, in turn,**

**enables deeper levels of interaction and
expression among team members.**

Trust building requires openness, information
sharing, honesty, and arguments; trust also enables
the free sharing of ideas, which is the basis of
innovation processes. Usually, the feeling of trust is
based on intuition and emotions.

High-performing teams have a clearly defined
and commonly shared purpose, mutual trust and
respect, clarity around individual roles and
responsibilities, high levels of communication,
willingness to work toward the greater good of the
team, and a leader who both supports and challenges
the team members. There is also a climate of
cooperation and an ability to voice differences and
appreciate conflict.

A high-performing team does not sweep
inevitable differences under the carpet and it values
openness. The importance of sharing personal
information, such as background, work experience,
and current organizational contexts, can't be
overstated.

Trust, benevolence, ability, and integrity are perceived to increase because of various team-building exercises. In high-trust teams, people express their feelings, e.g., excitement, more freely. Team members also give each other recognition and feedback. Disagreements are discussed more openly. Overall, high-trust teams have more open interaction and discussion.

Point Blank – Take Five

While difficult to describe, trust is tangible when experienced. In highly effective team workshops that I lead, I ask the participants exactly this question: How do we measure trustful experiences to ensure that it exists within the team? Initially, the notion of trust emerges from the team charter exercise. Participants easily define trust as a key ingredient of effective teams. They are quick to write on the flipcharts statements, such as "team members trust each other" or "team members and team leader exhibit trust in their activities" and also "a high performance team has should exhibit trust between team members."

*None of these definitions comes closer to
explaining how to measure trust. This is a* **common
challenge with soft components** *of team building. It is
straightforward to define the labels; it is difficult to
provide* **quantitative indicators for measuring the
level of interpersonal relationships, which exist
behind the labels.**

*I would like to share one of the best kept secrets of
training soft skills in general and high performance
team building specifically. This is the concept of
conduct objectives.*

*We define the conduct or behavior that
characterizes the label. In other words, we examine
what behaviors we are expecting to encounter if trust
exists. We can also define behaviors that, if increased,
would lead to more trust. By moving from generic
labels to specific measurable conduct, we give the team
an explicit tool to measure its progress in the otherwise
intangible soft components of relationships.*

Remember that trust is just a label. Make sure
you know how trust looks and feels. Measure it.

Must-Have #6:
Solve Problems and Make Effective Decisions

Nothing can put the brakes on a team effort faster than procrastinating on decision making. While high performance teams may use a variety of methods to arrive at their decisions, one thing is clear—they make decisions.

Whether the team arrives at the decision democratically or the individual with the most knowledge about that particular area makes the decision unilaterally, they make decisions in a timely manner and stick with them.

That is not to say that they never change a decision if necessary; however, unless they discover that a change is necessary, they stay with what they've decided. On the other hand, they are not so wedded to the decision that they won't change when necessary.

In essence, teams make decisions using problem-solving techniques. Thus, the process largely rests on the selection of a course of action following the evaluation of two or more alternatives. To effectively navigate this path, the following step-by-step approach can be used.

1. Recognize the problem

Teams must see and recognize that a problem exists and that a decision needs to be made to move forward. While on its face, this step appears elementary, many teams do not recognize that an issue needs to be addressed because of conductions such as groupthink (which will be discussed later).

2. Define the problem

In this stage, teams must map out the issue at hand. During this step, teams should:

- State how, when, and where members became aware of the problem;
- Explore different ways of viewing the problem; different ways of viewing the problem can lead to an improved understanding of the 'core' problem;
- Challenge any assumptions made about the problem to ensure that the team fully sees the 'real' issue at hand.

3. Gather information

Once the problem has been defined, teams need to gather information relevant to the problem.

Why do teams need to perform this step? First, to verify that the problem was defined correctly in step 2, and second, to develop alternative solutions to the problem at hand.

4. Develop alternative solutions

While it can be easy for teams to 'jump on' and accept the first solution, teams effective in problem solving take the time to explore several potential solutions to the problem.

5. Select the BEST alternative

Once all the alternatives are in, the team needs to determine the alternative that best addresses the problem at hand. For this element to be effective, team members need to consider both rational and human elements.

6. Implement the best alternative

Once the alternative has been chosen, the team needs to implement it. This requires effective planning and communicating the decision to all stakeholders that might be affected by this decision.

7. Evaluate the outcome

Remember that team building is a learning process. It is critical that the team examine, whether the proposed plans of action were achieved in an effective way and resulted in positive outcomes

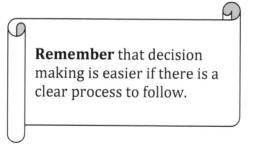

Remember that decision making is easier if there is a clear process to follow.

Must-Have #7:
Value and Promote Diversity

Often, the differences among individuals make them effective in what they do. Each one is able to bring their own viewpoint and abilities to the table, adding something that nobody else on the team can add. While small-minded people struggle with accepting those who are different, members of high performance teams accept and embrace the diversity of their co-members.

They count on that diversity to provide the ideas necessary, to create innovative solutions to problems.

This can only happen when each team member is willing to accept the others for who they are, without belittling them for what they aren't.

Most global teams are aware of cross-cultural diversity, and organizations are investing in training and coaching of the various aspects of cultural diversity.

Based on my experience from coaching and mentoring the development of high performance teams, I decided to highlight another type of diversity that is ever more apparent in contemporary teams, and when overlooked, it impedes the effectiveness of the team. I am referring to cross-generation diversity.

A mixed-generation team inevitably contains a diversity of perspectives and views, which if channeled well, can lead to the best solutions, the best products, and a highly engaged team. Get it wrong and it can mean conflict, ineffective work output, and a feeling of frustration among the team members.

Get it right, and you can release knowledge, wisdom, and talent from all generations. A great cross-generational team feels vibrant and a sense of learning and fun exists among the generations

What are the benefits of effective cross-generational teams?

Most organizations today are, by definition, a multi-generational group of people. Organizations would benefit from understanding how to get the most from their entire workforce, and to empower it to work productively together. Different generations working together can bring huge benefits to the individual, the team, and the organization. The

benefits listed below are as applicable to large teams
(entire organizations) as they are to small teams.

The specific benefits of effective cross-
generational teams include:

- **Increased insight into different customer
  age segments.** Bringing a range of perspectives
  to bear on an issue is important when working
  on topics that affect customers and individual
  consumers because it involves considering a
  range of ages/generations.
- **Improved knowledge sharing and
  knowledge management**. Organizations often
  struggle with how to capture and share the
  immense knowledge of the senior members of
  an organization. Mentoring is one way of doing
  this, as is cross-generational team working. The
  informal networking aspects of a dynamic team
  are also a fantastic medium for surfacing the
  knowledge and wisdom of its members.
- **Breaking down hierarchical and status
  barriers.** These barriers can be unhelpful when
  they inhibit open conversations, sharing, and
  healthy challenges. The more different

generations can understand about one another and work together, the more the barriers will be broken down.

- **Better solutions**. When people with diverse views and perspectives work together—provided they learn to listen to and work with diversity—they inevitably produce better solutions and products than homogeneous teams do.

How do the different generations work in teams?

Let's revisit the team styles and preferences of the different generations. It is important not to stereotype the different generations but, rather, to understand their perceptions and how they collaborate.

Baby boomers: (born 1946-1964)

- Team working style: Teamwork is about "pulling together" and "team spirit." Team meetings are scheduled at key points in a project (a planned approach).

- Value/style in teams: Must have common purpose, values, goals, etc. It's important that people "fit."
- Preferred teamwork medium: Face to face.
- Concerns/weaknesses: Tendency to defer to more senior team members.

Gen X: (born 1964-1980)

- Team working style: Value unique contributions. Team meetings are scheduled at key points in the project (a planned approach).
- Value/style in teams: Realize that diversity is good but sometimes struggle with it. Enjoy the networking aspects of teamwork.
- Preferred teamwork medium: Prefer face-to-face and know that virtual is needed, but are uncomfortable with it.
- Concerns/weaknesses: "Knowledge is power," i.e., they may be reluctant to share; individualistic and competitive tendencies.

Gen Y: (born 1981-2000)

- Team working style: Trust and openness is paramount. Want team meetings only when necessary: little and often.
- Value/style in teams: Like to know the bigger picture, the purpose. Diversity is exciting and challenging to them; it's an opportunity to learn. Status not an issue; they speak to the "person" not the "position."
- Preferred teamwork medium: Likes face-to-face and comfortable with virtual teamwork. Technology is an important tool for sharing, such as wikis, and communication "on-demand," such as instant messaging.
- Concerns/weaknesses: Can appear too "random" for Boomers and Xers and may need to receive coaching on project planning and formal feedback mechanisms. Can appear disrespectful to more senior team members.

Remember that different age groups tend to think differently; revel in the opportunities that diversity provides.

Must-Have #8:
Successfully Manage Conflict

In many cases, conflict in the workplace just seems to be a fact of life. We've all seen situations where different people with different goals and needs have come into conflict. And, we've all seen the often-intense personal animosity that can result. **The fact that conflict exists, however, is not necessarily a bad thing: As long as it is resolved effectively, it can lead to personal and professional growth.**

Effective conflict resolution can mean the difference between positive and negative outcomes.

The good news is that by resolving conflict successfully, you can solve many of the problems that it has brought to the surface, as well receive benefits you might not expect:

- **Enhanced group cohesion**: When conflict is resolved effectively, team members can develop stronger mutual respect and a renewed faith in their ability to work together.

- **Increased understanding**: The discussion needed to resolve conflict expands people's awareness of the situation, giving them an insight into how they can achieve their own goals without undermining those of other people.

- **Improved self-awareness**: Conflict pushes individuals to examine their goals in close detail, helping them to understand the things that are most important to them, sharpening their focus, and enhancing their effectiveness.

However, if conflict is not handled effectively, the results can be damaging. Conflicting goals can quickly turn into personal dislike. Teamwork breaks down. Talent is wasted as people disengage from their work. It's easy to end up in a vicious downward spiral of negativity and recrimination.

To keep your team or organization working effectively, this downward spiral needs to stop as soon as possible. To do this, it helps to understand two of the theories behind effective conflict resolution:

Theory: Conflict Styles of Kilmann

In the 1970s, Kenneth Thomas and Ralph Kilmann identified **five main styles of dealing with conflict that vary in their degrees of cooperativeness and assertiveness**. They argued that people typically have a preferred conflict resolution style. However, they also noted that different styles were most useful in different situations. They developed the Thomas-Kilmann Conflict Mode Instrument (TKI), which helps identify the style one is most likely to use when conflict arises.

Thomas and Kilmann's styles are:

Competing

People who tend toward a competitive style take a firm stand and know what they want. They usually operate from a position of power drawn from things like position, rank, expertise, or persuasive ability. This style can be useful when there is an emergency and a decision needs to be made fast, when the decision is unpopular, or when defending against someone who is trying to exploit the situation selfishly. However, it can leave people feeling bruised, unsatisfied, and resentful when used in less urgent situations.

Collaborating

People tending toward a collaborative style want to meet the needs of all people involved. These people can be highly assertive but, unlike the competitor, they cooperate effectively and acknowledge that everyone is important. This style is useful when bringing together a variety of viewpoints to reach the best solution, when there have been previous conflicts in the group, or when the situation is too important for a simple trade-off.

Compromising

People who prefer a compromising style wish to find a solution that will at least partially satisfy everyone. Everyone is expected to give up something and the compromiser also expects to relinquish something. Compromise is useful when the cost of conflict is higher than the cost of losing ground, when equal strength opponents are at a standstill, and when there is a deadline looming.

Accommodating

This style indicates a willingness to meet the needs of others at the expense of one's own needs. The accommodator often knows when to give in to others, but can be persuaded to surrender a position even when not warranted. This person is not assertive but is highly cooperative. Accommodation is appropriate when the issues matter more to the other party, when peace is more valuable than winning, or when you want to be in a position to collect on this "favor." However, people may not return favors and, overall, this approach is unlikely to give the best outcomes..

Avoiding

People tending toward this style seek to evade the conflict entirely. This style is typified by delegating controversial decisions, accepting default decisions, and not wanting to hurt anyone's feelings. It can be appropriate when victory is impossible, when the controversy is trivial, or when someone else is in a better position to solve the problem. However, in many situations, this is a weak and ineffective approach to take.

Once you understand the different styles, you can use them to reflect about the most appropriate approach (or mixture of approaches) for the situation you're in. You can also think of your own instinctive approach and learn how you need to change it if necessary.

Ideally, you can adopt an approach that meets the situation, resolves the problem, respects people's legitimate interests, and mends damaged working relationships.

Theory: The Interest-Based Relational Approach

The second theory is commonly referred to as the "Interest-Based Relational" (IBR) approach. **This type of conflict resolution approach respects individual differences while helping people avoid becoming too entrenched in a fixed position**.

In resolving conflict using this approach, you follow these rules:

- **Make sure that good relationships are the first priority**: As far as possible, make sure that you treat the other calmly and that you build mutual respect. Do your best to be courteous to one-another and remain constructive under pressure;

- **Keep people and problems separate**: Recognize that in many cases the other person is not just "being difficult"—real and valid differences can lie behind conflictive positions. By separating the problem from the person, real issues can be debated without damaging working relationships;

- **Pay attention to the interests being presented**: By listening carefully, you'll most-likely understand why the person is adopting his or her position;

- **Listen first, talk second**: To solve a problem effectively you have to understand where the other person is coming from before voicing your own position;

- **Set out the "Facts"**: Agree and establish the objective observable elements that will affect the decision;

- **Explore options together**: Be open to the idea that a third position may exist and that you can get to this idea jointly.

By following these rules, you can often keep contentious discussions positive and constructive. This helps prevent the antagonism and dislike that so-often causes conflict to spin out of control.

Using the Tool: A Conflict Resolution Process

Based on these approaches, a starting point for dealing with conflict is to identify the overriding conflict style employed by yourself, your team, or your organization. Over time, people's conflict management styles tend to mesh and a "right" way to solve conflict emerges. It's good to recognize when this style can be used effectively. Make sure people understand that different styles can suit different situations.

Look at the circumstances and think about the style that may be appropriate. Then, use the process below to resolve the conflict.

Step One: Set the Scene

If appropriate to the situation, agree the rules of the IBR Approach (or at least consider using the approach yourself). Make sure that people understand that the conflict might be a mutual problem, which may be best resolved through discussion and negotiation rather than through raw aggression.

If you are involved in the conflict, emphasize
that you are presenting your perception of the
problem. Employ and promote active listening skills
to ensure you hear and understand others' positions
and perceptions.

- Restate;
- Paraphrase;
- Summarize.

Make sure that when you talk, you're using an
assertive approach rather than a submissive or
aggressive style.

Step Two: Gather Information

Understand the underlying interests, needs, and
concerns. Ask for the other person's viewpoint and
confirm that you respect his or her opinion and need
his or her cooperation to solve the problem.
Appreciate his or her motivations and goals, and see
how your actions might be affecting these.

State the conflict in objective terms. Is it
affecting work performance? Damaging the delivery
to the client? Disrupting teamwork? Hampering

decision-making? Be sure to focus on work issues and **leave personalities out of the discussion**.

- Listen with empathy and see the conflict from the other person's point of view.
- Identify issues clearly and concisely.
- Use "I" statements.
- Remain flexible.
- Clarify feelings.

Step Three: Agree on the Problem

This sounds like an obvious step, but often, different underlying needs, interests, and goals can cause people to perceive problems differently. You'll need to agree on the problems that you are trying to solve before you'll find a mutually acceptable solution. Sometimes different people will see different but interlocking problems; if you can't reach a common perception of the problem, then at the very least, you need to understand what the other person sees as the problem.

Step Four: Brainstorm Possible Solutions

If everyone is going to feel satisfied with the resolution, it will help if everyone has had fair input in generating solutions. Brainstorm possible solutions and be open to all ideas, including ones you never considered before.

Step Five: Negotiate a Solution

By this stage, the conflict may be resolved. Both sides might have a better understanding of the other's position and a mutually satisfactory solution may be clear to all. However, you might also have uncovered real differences between your positions. Here, a technique like win-win negotiation can be useful to find a solution that, to some extent, satisfies everyone. There are three guiding principles: **Be Calm. Be Patient. Have Respect**

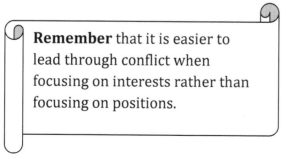

Remember that it is easier to lead through conflict when focusing on interests rather than focusing on positions.

Must-Have #9:
Provide Development
Opportunities and Recognition

While the team as a whole has goals for success, it recognizes that each team member needs opportunities to succeed in their own life and career. By helping team members find the opportunities to increase their individual skills and knowledge, they increase the ability of the overall team, increasing the team's probability for success.

Provide proper development and coaching. Whether through a formal 360-degree instrument or informal conversations, it is important to obtain feedback on areas of strength or developmental opportunities for all team members, and provide the training needed to enhance their performance. Team members require some level of coaching support to sustain new skills and reinforce new behaviors.

Plenty of research has been done to indicate that rewards and recognition, both monetary and non-monetary, play a significant role in encouraging desired behaviors from people. As such, be sure you have effective incentives in place to motivate and drive the kind of behavior you need from team members.

Don't make the mistake of incentivizing only cumulative results of a team—too frequently that will just drive a mediocrity. Think of the sales manager who steps in and just sells as an individual, or the software team leader who simply steps in and does the programming for a project. **Incentivize and recognize the leadership behaviors that make a qualitative difference** in performance, as well as quantitative results achieved. **Team members will take notice of what is valued and rewarded.**

Give team members the space to grow into the role. In addition to the tools and resources that you provide for them, they need—above all else—space. That is not to say that they don't need to perform effectively from the start or that you should give someone who is well below standards more chances than necessary.

Allowing team members cycles of learning, and the chance to continuously improve their abilities is probably the most predictable success factor of all.

Point Blank – Take Six

Remember to award incentives based on both personal achievement as well as team performance.

*Awarding incentives according to the **entire team performance might promote mediocrity**, where underperforming team members hide behind the highly performing ones. On the other hand, awarding incentives based solely on individual performance will break the high performance team and might lead to an overly competitive environment. **Recognition should be based on balanced indicators determined on individual contribution and contribution to the team performance**.*

———

It may seem difficult to make all these things happen with a virtual team, but actually, it isn't. While the challenge is real, it is possible to overcome it. More than anything, doing so requires effective communication between team members.

Remember to say thanks and to show gratitude; small gestures go a long way.

Trusted Communication, a Key to High Performance

As we've already discussed, high performance teams rely extensively on developing synergy. This is impossible without constant effective communication. While communications can be more challenging for a virtual team than for collocated teams, it's a challenge that can, and must, be overcome.

When a team is physically collocated, people tend to communicate on an informal basis. Team members interact with each other constantly, whether it is talking around the water cooler, running into each other in the hallways, or sitting together at lunch. Often, informal communication is the most effective because that is where many ideas are born. It's also the type of communication that lets team members get to know each other, so that they can meld together as a team and communicate more effectively.

On top of this informal communication, it is necessary to have regular formal meetings to keep everyone informed about the activities of other team members and to provide a forum to discuss problems and reach important decisions. Both formal communication and informal communication are necessary for the team to be effective; it doesn't work to have one without the other.

For a virtual team to become high performance, it must develop this same level of communication–not just formal communication, but informal communication as well.

Yet, in most cases, the only communication is formal during infrequent meetings. To become high performance, making this communication happen requires developing new communication methodologies utilizing the available technology.

The age in which we live has been dubbed the "information" age. Computer communications, especially through the Internet, has made it possible for individuals to communicate and share information around the globe.

Virtual teams must embrace this technology and make it work for them to make constant formal and informal communications possible.

There is no one formula for creating effective communication. Each virtual team will develop its own communication methods that work for it. What functions for one team might not work as well for another.

Nonetheless, it is essential that the communications protocols include both formal and informal communications. Regular meetings via Skype or Google Hangout provide an excellent format for virtual meetings. E-mail can be used for sending memos and reports to every team member, ensuring that they all have the latest information. Between these two, much of the formal communication can be addressed.

Even so, formal communication isn't enough; while it may seem like a waste of time, every virtual team must develop a method of informal communication as well. This is not a waste of time because **it is through the informal communications that team members get to know one another, developing the trust and comfort level necessary so that they can collaborate on ideas**.

Developing informal communications in a virtual team is a challenge. There is no coffee pot or water cooler for people to gather around. The traditional opportunities of coffee breaks, lunches, and even sitting in the conference room waiting for a meeting to start are eliminated. Hence, the team leader has to create virtual equivalents. Because no physical water cooler exists, there needs to be a virtual one, where team members can chat about their lives, families, politics, the weather, and even their work.

Fortunately, the Internet provides opportunities for this. Forming a group on Facebook or through Google Circles provides a way of creating this virtual water cooler. Just creating the group isn't enough, though; something has to be done to **kick-start conversation and act as an icebreaker**.

Adding times for team members to share their personal thoughts as part of formal communication is one way of doing this. Team members can take turns sharing a favorite quote to wrap up the meeting, have one meeting per week where everyone shares aspects of their lives, or one meeting per week discussing something that everyone has read or a video that everyone has seen. These activities will open the door for continued communication, especially if they are conducted through the virtual water cooler.

As team members communicate more through online meetings and using the virtual water cooler, they get to know one another better, communicate with one another more effectively, and anticipate each other's reactions and needs. This helps the overall mission by making it easier for the team to collaborate, rather than having people wander aimlessly.

———

Case Study Example #1

When Mark took over as the Mobile Software Development team leader, he faced a challenge. He had been given a team that was scattered across three countries and was as fragmented as could be. The core team at the company headquarters in Silicon Valley was well integrated, but they had to work together with team members in Poland and South Korea. This created huge challenges. There was nothing wrong with the individual team member's skills and proficiency, but communication between the core group and the extended team members was tenuous, at best.

This was Mark's first time as a team leader and he wanted to do it well. Somehow, he had to turn his fragmented team into a high performance team. The only question was ... how?

Before taking over the team, Mark spent a week in an intensive team leader's training seminar. He felt that he had a good grasp on how to make a strong team; he just wasn't sure how to do it over such long distances and with such diverse schedules. Somehow, he'd have to find a way to apply the principles that he had learned in that seminar to working with a virtual team, even though his team was scattered across thousands of miles and many time zones.

The first thing that Mark decided to do to turn his team around was to improve communications. That was going to be enough of a challenge in and of itself, but if he couldn't do that, then he wouldn't be able to do anything else.

To get his team's communication on track, Mark instituted mandatory team meetings. Because his team members were scattered, he used Skype for this. He felt that he needed to get everyone on the same page, and he also needed to get them to know one another. So, his meetings were a little bit different from the typical company meeting. Instead of spending all their time with boring status reports, he had everyone send their status report in so that it could be compiled on a weekly basis for all team members. Amanda, his team's technical writer, took care of that even though it wasn't really part of her job. She put together a standard format for everyone to use so that all she had to do was compile it and e-mail it out. That gave Mark the ability to use his team meetings as he wanted to, for team building, rather than for status updates.

Mark's team meetings became the most unusual ones in the company. Besides everyone giving a one-sentence summary of their day's work, the rest of the time was spent on getting to know one another. Each day, one of the team members, chosen at random, talked about himself or herself. Members gave a brief autobiography, answering a list of ten questions that the team had put together.

Each meeting ended with somebody sharing a favorite quote. It didn't matter where the quote came from or even if they made it up themselves; the idea was to share ideas that they could talk about later at the water cooler (more on that in a minute).

Friday's team meeting was different. Mark got his human resources coordinator, Julia, to put together an informal management training time. Each week, she'd send out a video or paper on some aspect of team building or management for everyone to review. Friday's meeting was spent discussing that, getting everyone's ideas and finding ways of applying what they learned to their team activities.

That took care of the formal communication, but Mark still needed to get the informal communication running. That's where the water cooler came in. It wasn't really a water cooler, but they called it that. It was the team's online forum where they could talk about different topics. Mark made it a team rule that everyone had to check the forum at least twice a day, and he encouraged the team members to comment regularly.

It took a while, but the water cooler ended up working out great. Threads would be posted about the words of wisdom that had ended the meeting. Other threads went up about people's personal problems, hobbies, and even pictures of their kids.

The surprising thing to Mark was that about half of the threads ended up being work-related. His team members started sharing what they were doing, bouncing ideas back and forth. The team was finally working together on ideas and problems even though they were operating across such vast distances.

Case Study Example #1 - Summary

Mark had taken the first step toward making his team high performance. By thinking outside the box and using the technology available to him, he found a way of drawing his team closer together, increasing their communication and getting them to work together.

- The increased communication that Mark instilled initiated relationship building;
- These relationships emerged through communications, and as they matured, they reciprocated in improved communications;
- By giving his team members the opportunity to learn about each other, he laid the foundation for those relationships to form;
- Mark's institution of the virtual water cooler and encouraging his team members to use it made the relationships blossom;
- The result was that the team was able to work together better, thereby accomplishing their goals.

As we have seen with Mark, team leaders are the ones who turn a team into a high performing one. While it is helpful to have motivated team members to work, much of a team's motivation depends on the leader. Mark started by getting his team talking to each other. While that won't make a team high performance all by itself, it's a good place to start.

Building a high performance team is a lot of work, especially for the team leader. But, as one manager said, it's a lot more work to not build a high performance team.

Some leaders consistently demonstrate the traits necessary to make their teams into high performance teams. They can be taken out of one team, dropped into another, and within 18 months, they'll have made the second team into a high performance team. Whether their old team remains high performance will depend on the leadership traits of the new team leader.

Reflect on your take-away from Mark's approach

Leadership Behaviors in a Highly Effective Team

More than anything, team leaders of high performance teams are visionary leaders. They don't start by looking at where their team is; they start by looking at where they want their team to be. Based on that, they work their way backward to figure out how to get there.

A vision is a picture of where you want to get to, not the path to get there. It's what the team will look like when it's reached its goal. But just having a vision isn't enough; the team leader must become infectious with the vision, getting the team to buy into it and make it their own. The vision may start with the leader, but it doesn't end there. That vision becomes the team's vision, not just the leader's vision.

Slogans are a great method to communicate visions—something short that encapsulates the vision and gives the team something to buy into. One of the best was created by Herb Kelleher, former CEO of Southwest Airlines. His vision, and the slogan that went with it, became the yardstick by which every decision in his corporation was made. Everyone from the boardroom to the back room understood that slogan and bought into the vision that it contained.

Kelleher's slogan was, "We are THE low-fare airline." You don't even have to be in the airline business to understand that; all you have to do is read it. New employees could have as much understanding of corporate culture and philosophy as the most experienced manager just by understanding that simple phrase. It captured the vision that Kelleher had for Southwest Airlines, making it something that everyone could buy into.

While not every vision is shared so eloquently, every leader should strive to do so. The clearer and more simply the vision is stated, the easier it is for team members to buy into it.

Be Genuine

High performance team leaders don't live in an ivory tower separated from their loyal subjects. They are part of the team and know when to open up and lower their guard with their team members. They aren't trying to project an image that they're perfect; they are willing to show their own vulnerabilities, especially if it can help another team member. This actually helps them gain the respect of their team, much more so than trying to appear flawless.

Exhibiting vulnerabilities requires self-confidence and being able to laugh at one's own mistakes. People who have to appear perfect often feel that way because they lack self-confidence. Yet, being willing to open up and be vulnerable can do more to make a team come together than standing aloof will.

Talk about Difficult Issues

Every team has difficulties; the question isn't whether they'll crop up, but how to deal with them when they do. Team leaders of high-performance teams recognize those difficulties and the problems behind them. They are willing to talk about the tough stuff, even though it's uncomfortable to do so. Their goal is always to work through the problem, gaining victory for the team.

Some leaders try to avoid conflict. All this does is make the problem fester, like an infection. That infection will eventually cause the team to become "sick" and dysfunctional. While nobody enjoys the conflict, going through it is essential.

One of the difficult things that leaders have to do is to confront non-performing team members. There are many reasons why a team member might not be performing up to expectations, and it's the leader's responsibility to find out the cause and do whatever is necessary to fix it. Sometimes, that means finding another team where the team member might fit in better.

That non-performing team member can sabotage the efforts of the entire team if not addressed. They may be the type of person who causes division, or who craves the limelight, or even one who rejects any leadership. Regardless of their problem, if it's not dealt with, it's like a plague eating away at the team.

Know How to Listen

Communication is a two-way street. Many leaders speak first and then, if there's time, they'll listen. Not so for team leaders of high performance teams. They know how to listen and generally listen to their team members before speaking. Remember, leadership in a high performance team is a collaborative effort. These leaders don't see themselves as "the boss" whom everyone is there to serve. They see themselves as facilitators, allowing their team to take its own direction.

An important part of this is listening. Everyone wants the opportunity to be heard, even the most junior member of the team. When these team leaders listen, they make the team members feel more important, as if their contributions are critical to the team.

Sometimes, it's not enough just to listen; the team leader has to get others to listen as well. A positive environment can't happen if team members are negative toward one another. It's the team leader's place to put an end to this as soon as it starts. Maybe the idea that a junior team member is putting forth won't work and won't be acted on, but they should be encouraged to express it nevertheless.

Ask Good Questions

Questions are a valuable tool. The right sort of questions can direct somebody to look in directions they never intended, to find the answers they so desperately need. Besides using questions to direct people, team leaders use questions to keep themselves abreast of what is happening in their team.

It has been said that because we have been given two ears and only one mouth, we should listen twice as much as we talk. Listening is an art form, and **asking questions is a tool to active listening**. Yet, asking a question without listening to the answer is one of the fastest ways of showing a team that you don't care about them. Good questions have to be followed by attentive listening.

Be Dependable

Good leaders have to be dependable. If the team is going to learn to depend on one another, it has to start with learning that it can depend on the leader. That means that the leader must carry through on whatever he or she says. If it proves impossible to complete what has been said, the leader must explain why or he or she will lose credibility in the eyes of the team.

People will do much more for a leader that they trust. In the military, one of the highest compliments an officer can receive, especially from an experienced sergeant, is "I'd be willing to follow you into battle." Whether we see it or not, our team's activities are a form of battle. We need our team members willing to follow us into that battle and win. That means that they have to trust us, which can only happen when we prove ourselves dependable.

Being dependable also means speaking clearly to team members. Most people can see right through a lot of the lies and misinformation that management passes out. While they may not be able to see what the truth is, they'll know the false when they see it.

Being honest with the team is another form of
dependability. It causes them to learn that they can
trust what you say and that you'll stand behind it.

Know How to Have a Good Time

Everyone likes to have a good time. That's a necessary part of team building. Leading a high performance team means leading them in having a good time together as well. However, they never do so at the expense of another person, especially another team member. Sarcasm and other cutting comments have no place in team fun because they have the potential to hurt somebody.

Having fun doesn't have to come at the expense of the team's goals. Many work activities can be made fun, and much of that has to do with how we approach those activities. If we approach them as something that we're going to do together as a team, we set the tone for making them fun.

Be Goal Oriented

Goals are the compass that directs the team. Regardless of what team activities are being undertaken, a high performance team leader keeps them goal oriented. It may be the team's ultimate goal or intermediate goals that will help the team reach that ultimate goal; it's still a goal and the team leader will keep it in focus. They'll also ensure that their team keeps it in focus.

This doesn't mean that the leader has tunnel vision. Team-building activities may seem to some like a waste of time, but those team-building activities are necessary to forge the team into a high performance team. Therefore, including them in the team's work schedule is helping the team reach its goals

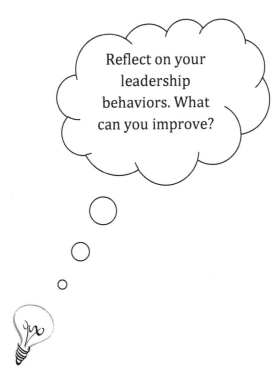

Maintaining Accountability across the Miles – The Virtual Challenge

One of the hardest parts of managing any team—let alone one that is scattered across the world—is maintaining accountability. Many people see a lack of direct supervision as an opportunity to have an extended semi-vacation with pay. They do some level of work to make sure they have something to report to their team leader, but they don't do the level of work they are being paid for or the level of work they are capable of.

The key to avoiding this problem is to hire the right sort of people. That can be challenging when hiring across the Internet, as direct communication can be difficult. It's hard to look somebody in the eye to see if they're telling the truth, when the only image you have of them is a tiny webcam image. This doesn't mean that all is lost though.

The greatest test of someone's work ethic isn't what they say in the interview, it's what they do when they think nobody is looking. Those are the times when people are most likely to log hours that they spend surfing the net or checking their e-mail, rather than doing their work.

Many people forget that there is always a probationary period when a new employee is hired. During this time, the supervisor has the option of terminating them without any risk. While employers tend to keep track of this for in-house employees, they are much more likely to forget about it for long-distance ones. However, if anything, it is more applicable for those who are in other countries.

Team leaders must have a good idea of how much time it should take for their team members to complete their tasks. The human resources department can help with this, along with the company's industrial engineers. Time standards have been created for almost any type of work, and while some types of work are more likely to have variances for time taken, those variances should balance out overall.

High-Performance People for High-Performance Teams

Any team leader who builds a high-performance team is selective about the people who stay on the team. There are people who just don't work out on the team, either through their lack of commitment, lack of knowledge, or poor work ethic. It really doesn't matter so much what the reason is, the team leader must be able to recognize these people and move them off the team.

This may require finding another position for that team member, especially if they have been with the company for a long time. New team members, or those who are hired as contractors, are easy to dismiss, but letting a long-standing employee go from a company is a more complicated operation.

Most of the time, it's the attitude, not the aptitude, that makes a person unsuitable for working on a high performance team. Generally speaking, employers hire aptitude rather than attitude. Just because a potential employee has all the right degrees, all the right references, and all the right knowledge, doesn't mean that they'll perform in all the right ways. Sometimes, those highly qualified people can be problems, expecting the world, or at least the team, to rotate around them.

On the other hand, a person with the right attitude will make up for their lack of aptitude. If they don't know something, they'll learn it. If they have never done it before, they'll jump in with both feet and try. Their attitude will cause them to excel, because they won't settle for anything less.

These type of people will take hold of the team's vision and run with it. While they may make mistakes along the way, they will make up for those mistakes through their hard work and coming up with the occasional brilliant "out of the box" idea. Ultimately, their value to the team will be much more than the "expert" who doesn't really care.

Remember, for a high-performance team to work, everyone on the team needs to buy into the team's vision. Ultimately, that will accomplish more than each team member's innate ability, as the synergy of the team will multiply everyone's ability.

Another aspect of these highly motivated workers is that they don't need direct supervision. They don't need somebody watching to see if they are working because they are watching themselves. They don't need to punch a time clock because they're working more hours than they're being paid for without even telling the boss. They are self-policing because of their enthusiasm.

———

Case Study Example #2

When Nigel was hired as the company's IT Manager, it was with the mandate of providing IT service to the company's clients around the world. He knew that this would be a challenge and require a highly motivated, highly effective team of people. The first thing that Nigel noticed when he was brought in as IT Manager and team leader was the fragmentation of his team. He had people working in six different countries, in almost as many time zones. Three of local sub-teams were led by people who thought they should have been given his job. He was in trouble.

To turn his team around, Nigel needed to break people out of their comfort zones and challenge them with a new standard. That's where he started. The vision he created set an entirely new standard for customer service, higher than the company had ever experienced before. Even so, he was confident he could achieve it, as long as he could get the team to trust him and work with him.

To overcome the bickering and dissent in his team, Nigel decided that he was going to have to *make a whirlwind tour of his various sub-teams, allowing the people to get to know him as he presented his new vision to them. This wasn't easy; he had to confront the problems that he saw head on, especially the dissention with the more experienced team members.*

What turned the tables for him was that he didn't think that he knew all the answers. While he confronted the bad attitudes that he ran across, he spent more time listening to his various scattered team members, getting their ideas for accomplishing the vision he had given them.

Nigel was flooded with ideas. Never before had anyone asked the sub-teams for their thoughts. Everything had been mandated from the central office, causing many of the bad attitudes he had inherited. By listening to them, he was able to make every team member feel that they were a valuable part of the team, that he valued their input, and that he wanted to work with them, rather than lord over them.

In addition to ideas, Nigel found out about a number of real problems that were making it hard for his team to work together. Instead of just listening to the teams complain about the problems, though, he asked for their solutions.

That was the turning point for Nigel's team. He had challenged them to do better and given them the opportunity to do so. He had shown that he was willing to listen to them, and that he valued their input. The same team members who had been the biggest complainers before suddenly became the biggest assets to the team. Nigel was overjoyed and when he implemented their suggestions, they were as well.

Case Study Example #2 Summary

Nigel needed to develop new systems for his team to use. Actually, he didn't so much develop these systems as find out the ideas that his team members had for changing or replacing the existing systems. The team had been trying to operate with systems that were designed for a collocated team, even though they were spread over half the world.

It doesn't matter how big the organization is or what it does, when the central office mandates everything, it often **mandates what is best for the central office**, not considering what will work well for the other team assets. With a virtual team, one has to consider the differences in culture, language, availability of materials, and educational level. Culture and the way that people live will play a major part in their ability to accomplish what the home office wants.

When part of the team is located in third world countries, regular services aren't necessarily reliable. Telephone and electrical service can go down and do so rather often. Team members may not be able to work simply because of a lack of electricity.

These types of problems must be considered when developing a virtual team. If the team is made up of contractors, they may need equipment they can't afford. While the average American wouldn't think anything of having to buy a mouse or keyboard for a computer, a worker in the Philippines may not be able to afford to do so. Not only are they working for a lower salary, but that keyboard is considerably more expensive.

Systems that require the whole world signing off on something are extremely difficult to implement in a virtual team. A simple manufacturing change is easy to implement if everyone's office is at the factory. But if the purchasing department is in one place, the design engineering department in another, the planning department in a third, with the manufacturing engineering department located at the factory, just trying to get the documents to everyone for signature can be complicated.

The use of online documents, databases, and virtual signatures makes this job easier. But, company policies must be adapted to the needs of the virtual

team, not the team adapted to the needs of the
company policies.

Shared Leadership

By probing the problems and suggestions of his
scattered team members, Nigel started the process of
shared leadership. Shared leadership doesn't
eliminate a team leader; rather, it involves everyone
in the decision-making process. Everyone in the team
ends up buying into the vision, goals, and systems
because they feel as if they had a part in creating
them.

A team leader may delegate leadership functions
to team members. A common way of doing this is by
using a roster to rotate the leadership of team
meetings. This gives everyone a chance to run the
meeting, helps train them for leadership, and takes
some of the burden off the team leader. Often, one
team member or another will have an idea for a
change in the meeting when they are chairing it,
which then becomes adopted by the whole team.

Another way that a team leader can involve team
members in leadership is to delegate them areas of
responsibility. Mark delegated a professional

development task to Julia, his human resources coordinator, having her take charge of the management development sessions they had on Fridays. On one hand, she assisted him in her role as a human resources coordinator; on the other hand, he was sharing the leadership role with her.

The same could be said for Nigel through his utilization of the senior team member in each country as sub-team leaders. While he still was the IT manager, he gave them autonomy and decision-making authority. This went a long way toward overcoming the resentment at his being hired, but even more importantly, it co-opted those team members into being committed to the team.

———

People will always put more effort into something that they think they have created. Typically, the hardest working people are those who are self-employed. They have built their business and they reap the benefits directly.

On a team, each member needs that same sense of ownership. While they may not actually own stock in the company, they can still gain that feeling of ownership by being involved in the decision-making process. This should start as early as possible, preferably as soon as the team is formed.

While the core objectives of the team will often be assigned to it, the vision and systems that bring about that objective are not. If the team leader creates those and presents them to the team, they will probably be accepted and used. However, if the team leader brings the team members into the process of creating them, they will be more than used—they will be the team's property. Team members will defend that vision, like a mother bear over her cubs, because it is theirs.

Reflect on your take away from Nigel's approach

Unique
Step By Step Guide
for a Two Day
High Performance
Team Workshop

As I have written in the preface to the third edition, in this chapter I am sharing with you my trainer notes for creating a high performance team. It is a workshop I have been delivering often, 55 times to date. The participants love it; engaging and intense, groups start at 8:00 the first day and by 18:00 the next, they are on the track to become a high performance team. Naturally, it is only the initiation of the process, and the magic must be retained through ongoing mentoring. However, it is a powerful jumpstart that yields amazing results.

Feel free to use it with your teams, in entirety or parts of it. You'll be amazed with the results.

Two Day Workshop – Overview, Objectives and Style

The learning need is for an intact team to be facilitated through a process whereby they refine and agree upon their collective objectives, agree upon how they will work together to achieve the objectives, and to learn skills that will enable them to interact best in the achievement of those objectives.

At the end of the workshop the team should be able to:

- Describe the constituents of a "high performing" team; assess their own team's effectiveness;
- Understand their objectives in an aligned manner; have clarity on their role within the team; agree on ways of working going forward;
- Apply basic influencing techniques (process definition as well as skills practice);
- Understand and agree on techniques to manage conflict (process definition as well as skills practice);

- Apply a range of communication techniques to support effective teamwork (process definition as well as skills practice);
- Assess team effectiveness and take/ recommend the appropriate actions; make more efficient use of team time.

The workshop is designed to encourage participation from all team members by providing a setting in which all the participants can contribute. Thus creating an opportunity to give and share their views and opinions in a seniority free environment. A range of creative exercises and team activities will be employed together with relevant theories, models, tools and techniques to bring to life the themes and topics of the workshop. There will be an opportunity to take part in team activities as well as interpersonal skills exercises and receive feedback on performance. There will be time allowed throughout the day for personal reflection.

The role of the facilitator will be to lead short theory based sessions to set the scene for the team, and lead into discussion groups, activities and exercises. The facilitator will work with the team and individuals to expand their understanding of how their team operates and enhance individual interpersonal skills.

The participants will receive a workbook which will contain the core themes and topics and enable participants to record their thoughts, ideas and progress through the two days. All the tools, templates and models will be contained within the book. **Processes will be added by the trainer.**

The participant book isn't part of this guide and can be purchased separately. Contact me for details.

Pre-Workshop Tasks

To assist participants consider the current team performance and prepare information for use within the workshop, the following activities should be individually completed. As a facilitator it is your role to ensure they have read the material specifically when the pre-course work is used within the training.

Activity One

Draw up a personal list of 10 criteria for developing a high performing team.   Your criteria can consist of actions, activities or behaviors that will lead to the development of a high performing team.

Activity Two

Consider your team and develop a list of three things the team members need to consider under the following headings: What does the team need to keep and continue? What to give up and stop? What to add and take up? To become a High performing team.

Activity Three

Prepare and write out what you believe to be your team's: direction; key tasks and objectives that bring to life the team purpose.

Activity Four

Prepare a team analysis to help you and your
colleagues consider the roles within the team and
your contribution to the team. Consider the
challenges you face and the support you require.

Activity Five

Read documentation provided that will contain
background reading for the modules on Influencing
and Conflict Handling.

Activity Six

Select a real life scenario that involves influencing /
handling conflict to use in a practice session.

1: Introductions

Purpose: Welcome and overview of the two days. To assist participants settle into the workshop and give the facilitator an opportunity to get to know the participants.

Objectives:

- Describe the constituents of a "high performing" team; assess their own team's effectiveness;
- Understand their objectives in an aligned manner; have clarity on their role within the team; agree on ways of working going forward;
- Apply basic influencing techniques (process definition as well as skills practice);
- Understand and agree on techniques to manage conflict (process definition as well as skills practice);
- Apply a range of communication techniques to support effective teamwork (process definition as well as skills practice);
- Assess team effectiveness and take/recommend the appropriate actions; make more efficient use of team time.

Instructions:

Welcome to the Workshop, Setting the scene for the two days to cover: Domestics - Fire alarm; break times and lunch time for the group; toilets; smoking rules; mobile phones & messages and finish time.

Outcomes – outline the outcomes of the workshop. Use the outcomes slides to give an overview of what is to be achieved within the two days.

Emphasize that the two days are about the team and the role of the trainer is to guide, coach and assist. There is a little training but overall this is a team workshop not tutor led training course.

Ice breaker exercise – use the following or any other from your toolbox:

Suppose you are stranded on a remote island. Divide to three teams and decide what *four** items you *would have brought with you*, had you known that you were going to be stranded for an extended period of time. NOTE: Each team is only allowed one item per person. So, the number of items will vary, depending on the total number of participants per team. *This exercise assists teams to learn about one another's values. It also promotes teamwork and fosters collaborative problem solving.*

2: Core Interpersonal Skills

Purpose: recognize the core interpersonal skills the team will use during the workshop.

Note: Team works together; trainer facilitates and assists as required.

Instructions:

Discussion – how to make the most of the workshop?

What can be included in a Team Charter?

- Team Agreement and Rules for operating over the next two days and beyond;
- The Charter can include team and individual behaviors;
- Also the things which the team values.

The team works together to discuss and agree a list of team / individual skills for the two days so all team members are able to play an active role in the workshop.

The team completes the team charter poster which will act as a reminder of the skills they have agreed to employ throughout the workshop to help the two days run smoothly.

Deliverable: Recognition of core interpersonal skills used in High Performing Teams.

Handout – Team Charter:

Why develop a team charter?

- Develops a common understanding of how team members will support each other;

- Builds the foundation for working together;

- Understand how each person can contribute to the team's success.

What can be included in a team charter?

- Team Agreement and Rules for operating (ground rules)

- Shared Vision and Goals

- Team Values and Beliefs

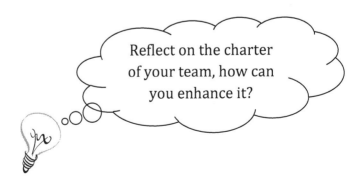

Reflect on the charter of your team, how can you enhance it?

3: Introducing the Roadmap and Team Model

Purpose: introduce team model and understand the roadmap to a high performance team.

Instructions:

Trainer led session with an opportunity to ask questions. Trainer will check the knowledge level of the participants regarding the team model and adjust input accordingly.

Explain and emphasize **team model**, as it will be referenced throughout the two days:

- Charter
- Team roles
- Trust
- Relationships
- Leadership

Trainer should understand the team model and relate to it. Make sure participants understand it and have enough knowledge to use it.

Road map for developing a "High Performing Team" – outline the four steps and emphasize that we will use the four steps as a basis for our workshop:

Step one: Understanding - what is a high performing team?

Step two: Purpose and direction – How are we to achieve our objectives?

Step three: Personal contribution – my role in team success?

Step four: Team process – How we interact together? How we influence each other and manage conflict?

Timing – one hour has elapsed

4: Effective Team Collaboration

Purpose: understand what a high performance team is and the actions to develop it. Learn the five elements team model. Use of pre-workshop task #1: Draw up a personal list of 10 criteria for developing a high performing team.

Note: This is a facilitated session

Instructions:

Start by telling the participants that this is an activity aimed at step one of high performing teams: What is a high performing team? We all have our own ideas; however the key is: how will you know when you have achieved the status of a high performing team?   What will the evidence be?

This activity is also linked with the pre-workshop task #1 which asked participants to "Draw up a personal list of 10 criteria for developing a high performing team".

The team works together to define: Effective high performing team working. To agree by consensus a set of 10 criteria for high performing teams. The criteria can consist of actions, activities or behaviors that will lead to the development of a high performing team.

Resources are: Utilizing the participants' individual pre-workshop tasks: Draw up a personal list of 10 criteria for developing a high performing team.

The team completes the exercise in ~30 minutes. Team needs to work on consensus without voting.

Trainer – **observes the team interactions and writes evidence/fact base observations**. He can use the Rackham & Morgan Interpersonal categories analysis as the basis for observations.

Part one review – Content delivered:

Focus on the content "What the team has produced by way of a substantial and powerful criterion to take forward".

Review of the teams criteria against the effectiveness of high performance teams: team purpose; team objectives; team process; team communication; team involvement and team

commitment. Comment if they have the main items
included in their criteria

Ask specific questions relating to **team model**:
Have they included elements around team purpose,
clear direction, roles, objectives, processes,
monitoring, open communications, support.

Remember team model?

- Charter;
- Team roles;
- Trust;
- Relationships;
- Leadership.

It may also be relevant to be familiar with the Hay
group model: 5 fundamentals of teams:

- Compelling Direction;
- Structure and Norms;
- People Skills;
- Support and Compensation;
- Development.

Deliverables:

- Know what actions to take to develop an effective team;
- Learn the five prime steps to team effectiveness – Hay Model.

Handout – highly effective teams:

Groups	Teams
Members work independently.	Members work interdependently.
Members focus exclusively on their own objectives.	Members focus on team and personal objectives.
Objectives are directed from above.	Objectives are established collaboratively.
Members operate outside the decision-making process.	Members are actively involved in the decision-making process.
Members form cautious, formal, selective relationships.	Members form trusting, supportive, informal relationships.
Conflict is regarded as negative and destructive.	Conflict is regarded pragmatically as a learning opportunity.

5: Process Review – Extremely Important

Purpose: To increase capability in recognizing and using interpersonal skills.

Note: This is a facilitated session.

Part two review – Team process:

Commentary: quick recap on the criteria the team produced and substantiate the steps required to produce a High Performing Team.

Explain that we will now have a **process review** to consider: How they ran the meeting and the processes the team used. Although this was an activity, they were actually in a meeting as they had an objective and outcome to achieve within a time frame.

First consider: Meeting protocol:

Ask: How did the team run the meeting? What worked well? Not so well?

Trainer to use flipchart to record the teams responses and help create a meeting

protocol <u>for example</u>: Did they have an agenda? <u>For</u> <u>example</u> was the task broken down into segment: how they would share information, how much time they would spend on gathering information, how much time on selecting the appropriate criteria, how they would make decisions regarding priority order.

Team should recognize that they have a meetings protocol or otherwise have it recorded or generate a meetings protocol with the help of the trainer.

Trainer records information on flipchart for team to take away.

Second: Decision making:

Ask: How were decisions made? What worked? What did not work? There are only four clear ways to make decisions:

- The leader, after gathering the facts;
- Team to vote - quick but not all will agree;
- Team to use consensus – slow with all getting a say and contribution;
- Decision making tool - Decision making matrix.

Commentary: the team needs to know how a specific decision will be made and the part they will play in the decision

The deliverable here is that the team need to be aware of the decision making processes and options they can use.

Behavioral Categories:

The trainer will briefly outline the twelve interpersonal categories and ask the team which of the Rackham and Morgan categories were used most during the activity (meeting).

The trainer will reveal the teams profile score showing how many **times each interpersonal category was used during the exercise and the impact this had on the team**.

Team review how effectively they worked together using the Interpersonal Categories and consider:

- What worked well? Which positive categories were used most?

- What did not work so well? Which positive categories were not used and how many of the negative categories?

Trainer note – extra information on Rackham and Morgan interpersonal categories:

- Proposing = Neutral, as too many will confuse the group. Action would be to encourage a few but have these of high quality. *Required few high quality;*
- Building = Positive and should be encouraged. *Required high number;*
- Supporting = Positive and should be encouraged. *Required high number;*
- Disagreeing = Neutral as it will be negative if there is no alternative or reason for the disagreement. If reasons are given then this will become more positive. *Required a few but high quality reasons;*
- Blocking = Always negative and needs to be discouraged. *Required none;*
- Defending /Attacking = Always negative and needs to be discouraged. *Required none;*

- Bringing in = Positive and needs to be encouraged. *Required as many as needed, but hopefully not too many as it will indicate some are not taking part;*
- Shutting out = Always negative and needs to be discouraged. *Required none;*
- Checking = Positive as it will help the group to keep aware of what is being discussed. *Required as many as is required;*
- Summarizing = Positive as recap on key points. *Required from time to time;*
- Seeking information = Positive as it acts as an enquiry and encourages others. *Required as many as is needed;*
- Giving information = Neutral if limited and focused it is positive but if egos are running away then negative. *Required good to see the number match the number of proposals, as a guide.*

Deliverables:

- Increase capability in recognizing and using interpersonal skills;

- Learn the Rackham & Morgan Template for use in the team.

Timing – 3 hours so far have elapsed

6: Evaluating the Challenge

Purpose: Relate to pre-workshop task two - Consider your team and develop a list of three things the team members need to consider under the following headings: What to continue? What to give up and stop? What to add and take up?

Objectives:

- Describe the constituents of a "high performing" team; assess their own team's effectiveness;
- Appreciate the team processes used at present and consider how they need to change.

Instructions:

Reviewing the current team performance to ensure criteria for a successful High Performance team is achieved.

Use the flipchart to brief the team

- Review current team performance against criteria for success (this is the output from the exercise 10 criteria for high performing teams);

- What actions, activities and behaviors do we want to continue?

These are the actions and activities that support the criteria produced. <u>For example</u>: "we will continue to set objectives or we will continue to hold monthly team meetings to aid communications."

- What actions, activities and behaviors do we want to stop?

These are the actions and activities that detract from or hinder reaching their criteria. <u>For example</u>: "we need to stop spending so much time debating issues and not making decisions, or we need to stop holding so many meetings, or we need to stop arguing over key responsibilities."

- What actions, activities and behaviors do we want to add or take up?

These are actions or activities than need to be started to achieve their criteria. <u>For example</u>: "We need to open the channels of communications or we need to agree team objectives or we need to develop more team processes."

**The issues priority is agreed by the team and
recorded on flipchart to take back to the
workplace.**

Trainer to facilitate a **process review based on
meeting protocol and decision making**. Did they
follow any meeting protocol? Did the team make clear
decisions?

Deliverable: Appreciate the team processes used at
present and consider how they need to change.

7: **Purpose and Direction**

Purpose: understand Level two: Purpose and direction – How are we to achieve our objectives?

Objectives:

- To agree on the team direction; key tasks and task objectives;
- To be able to apply the Hay Theory within the workplace.

Relates to pre-workshop task activity three: Prepare and write out what you believe to be your teams: direction; key tasks and objectives that bring to life the team purpose.

Instructions:

Hay Group – team model links with the Team Charter Activity completed previously. (Short trainer led session on the Hay Group.)

Trainer to brief the team on the activity and to facilitate a discussion, where individual team members can openly discuss their views on team direction, key tasks and task objectives.

Note: The participants will have started this activity within their pre-workshop tasks, so this is merely combining the information.

The activity can be conducted in small groups of three or four. The task is to: Produce a flipchart page that clearly indicates the team's direction = in this case Purpose, What is the team here to do?

To achieve the Purpose, What are the Key Tasks they need to achieve? **Key tasks need to be defined in terms of task objectives**

Groups work to produce a flipchart that outlines the team's direction, key tasks and task objectives.

Review: assemble the small groups together and display the flipcharts and compare and contrast the purpose, key tasks and objectives produced by the teams, and facilitate a discussion to agree with the team the purpose, key tasks and task objectives.

Emphasize the need for effective team processes. For example: meeting protocol, decision making and monitoring of team performance as essential for effective team work and time control.

Deliverables:

- A team agreement on the team direction; key tasks and task objectives;
- Be able to apply the Hay Theory within the workplace.

8: Task Objectives

Purpose: to have clarity on their role within the team; agree on ways of working, moving forward. To ensure that the team objectives are aligned with the following model:

- Objective is easily understood;
- Objective can be managed;
- The conditions exist that will lead to success and achievement;
- The objective helps attain team or business unit targets;
- Time frames for the objective have been identified.

Instructions:

Outline the two types of objective: **Task** and **conduct**.

Small groups each take a number of the team objectives and ensure the objective complies with the illustrated model above.

Team displays objectives for a critique session.

Within the small groups the teams consider what the other teams have produced and if necessary make suggestions to improve the quality of the objectives. Emphasize the use of objectives within the team and for monitor purposes.

Deliverable: Ability to create precise objectives to aid monitoring of performance.

9: Conduct Objectives – Extremely Important!

Purpose: Apply a range of communication techniques to support effective teamwork and learn to use Conduct objectives:

Instructions:

Team reviews the team charter and agrees the most important items they need to use to achieve the team task objectives. The team agrees their top four items / values and then brings them to life through the development of conduct objectives, to help monitor team performance and build personal commitment.

For example they may have written: Support each other or ensure we use the time effectively. **The team then needs to produce conduct objectives to ensure these valued ways of conducting themselves are captured so they can be monitored.**

Trainer led session on Conduct Objectives

Short session on conduct objectives – creating clear conduct objectives to ensure all participants understand the process.

If appropriate the trainer to take one of the teams values <u>for example</u>: "we support each other during time of pressure and develop with the team the positive and negative conduct behaviors."

Activity Briefing - Produce the four conduct objectives.

The trainer to brief the team on the next activity which involves the creation of conduct objectives so the team can monitor their conduct against the objectives.

Trainer to facilitate the activity.

The team draft Conduct Objectives to ensure the skills are used and monitored within the team

Deliverable:

- Learn to use Conduct objectives
- Individuals commit to using the agreed skills

Handout - Creating Clear Conduct Objectives:

'Conduct Objectives' are objectives that are qualitative, i.e. harder to measure by numbers, or single specific outcomes. They are very useful for team development and helping teams focus on what behaviors are needed to succeed.

- To create clear conduct objectives requires you to be able to identify two types of outcomes associated with the objective :
  - Skills or conduct you do want to see happening as a 'measure' of this objective being achieved ;
  - Skills or conduct you don't want to see happening – or if they occur, it shows that the objective is not being met.
- To check achievement you need to watch and talk to others because success is based on what you see and hear.

- o Outcomes you do want to see are known as 'positive indicators' ;
- o Outcomes you don't want to see are known as 'negative indicators'.

Here is an example of a Conduct Objective

Objective: To be an effective team member

Positive Indicators	Negative Indicators
• Shares knowledge and ideas with others	• Keeps ideas to self and does not offer views in meetings
• Helps others out when they are in trouble	• Refuses to get involved – sees it as the other person's problem or issue
• Gives honest, open and helpful feedback	• Only gives negative views of the team and sees problems rather than solutions
• Keeps colleagues informed of any issues or problems that may impact the team	• Sees knowledge as power and does not share information
• Questions and asks others when unsure of what action to take	• Does not ask for help or support when under pressure

10: Role Clarity within the Team

Purpose: to understand **Step three**: Personal contribution – my role in team success.

Pre-workshop task four: My Role in the high performing team. Individuals consider their role and contribution to the team and complete the Team Analysis.

Instructions:

Individual Activity and shared results.

Trainer outlines Team Analysis.

Participants prepare for the exercise using the post it notes to record the information they will share with the team.

Trainer to facilitate a discussion where each member of the team has a turn at describing their role within the team.

- My role within the team: Indicate your role and key responsibility within the team;
- Challenges: Challenges you face with your role and responsibilities;

- Support: Support that other team members can give to help you overcome the challenges.

The trainer will need to ensure each person has a turn and that the team challenges and supports each other on the issues and come up with workable solutions to the issues raised.

Ensure that there is a discussion and awareness raising about the different ways a team can function, i.e. leader needs to take decisions, leader can delegate expertise (and decision guidance) to a team member, team members may work on their own or in small groups as subject matter experts before reporting back to whole team, team may need to work as a whole unit on some activities, etc.

Deliverable:

- Appreciate the roles within the team and how the team can challenge and support each other.

11: Recap and Commitments

Purpose: To review the day learning and generate a personal action plan to implement at work.

Instructions:

Development of individual action plans and commitments to develop the high performing team.

Facilitated discussion.

Trainer to set up the activity using template: Personal application planning.

Allow the participants individual reflection time before facilitating a discussion on their personal action plans.

Deliverable:

A personal action plan to monitor.

End of first day

12: Review and Set the Stage – Second Day

Purpose: To ensure participants are in a receptive mode.

Instructions:

Trainer lead session. Consider using a short ice breaker or energizer to get thing on the move.

Review of previous day material and learning. Trainer facilitates an interactive session to discuss the learning from previous day.

Trainer will also focus on the team analysis exercise from the previous day, to ensure all issues involving the challenges and support required have been covered.

Preview of the upcoming workshop material – set the scene for day two of the workshop.

13: Team Interactive Exercise

Purpose: Putting the ideas into practice, to consolidate day one skills, tools and templates.

Instructions:

Building a Television Tower – Team Game

- Divide the team into three equal teams. Brief the team on the activity using a handout;
- The participants will take part in an interactive exercise working in small teams;
- Each team will select a leader and the trainer will brief the leader who will in turn brief their team;
- Teams will start to plan and build their towers.

The trainer will issue another set of guidelines after about 10 minutes into the exercise, instructing the teams that they now have to collaborate to win the exercise.

Trainer to observe the teams and note the positive and negative behaviors and the processes they are using for the consecutive review.

<u>The trainer conducts a review:</u>

Team members will complete team process review in their workbook for the team they worked in. Then review the team performance. They will report back to whole group.

Conduct a facilitated discussion with the entire team regarding the learning from the exercise.

Note: During the review ensure each team had an objective that they could measure themselves against. Also verify that their team behaviors matched against the conduct objectives and skills used were aligned with the positive Rackham and Morgan - Interpersonal Categories.

Deliverable:

Consolidation of day one skills, tools and templates

Timing – 2 hours so far have elapsed

14: Influencing Skills in High Performance Teams - Theory

Purpose: To understand the need for a clear process when working with influencing skills.

Objectives:

- Understand the way we influence each other and manage conflict;
- To examine influencing styles and explore the appropriate use of each style.

Reference:

Step four: Team process – How we interact together? How we influence each other and manage conflict?

Pre-workshop task five: Read documentation provided that will contain background reading for the modules on Influencing and Conflict Handling.

Instructions:

Influencing styles – push and pull styles

Trainer led session and discussion using pre-course work.

Review the range of styles and discuss the styles individuals use most.

Influencing: The Styles and Skills

ENERGY	STYLE	SKILLS	WORDS
Push	Persuading	Proposing	"I propose… I suggest… It would be a good idea if…"
		Reasoning	"For the following two reasons…"
Push	Asserting	What you want/need	"I want you to… I need you to… I expect you…"
		Direct feedback	"I like the way you… I don't like the way…"
		Incentives/Pressures	"If you do this: then I will…" *Incentive*
			"If you do this: then I will…" *Pressure*
Pull	Involving	Encouraging	"You have good ideas on this Jim. What's your view?"
		Listening	"It seems to me that what you are saying is…"
		Sharing Feelings	Content, Meaning, Feeling
			"I am excited about what you say… I am concerned… I feel uncertain… I don't feel easy with our discussion…"
Pull	Inspiring	Painting a picture	"Imagine…", "I can see…", "The picture I have of where we are going is…"
			See, Hear, Feel
		Common Interests	"What we have in common is …", "What we agree on is …"
Reduce	Withdrawing	Disengaging	"I need to have time to think on your proposals…"
		Opting out	"This is getting too heated, let's take a break."

Conduct the influencing Quiz drawn from background reading activity.

Divide into two teams

Ask the team to write Energy / Styles / Skills on a flipchart. Then ask them to compete by writing the appropriate words from the pre-workshop reading under the appropriate headings.

Teams and individuals within the teams need to be conscious of how the team members influence each other as a team develops and grows.

Ask the team which styles are used the most within the team and ask individuals which style they use.

Ask which styles of influencing each, participant use: Push and Pull styles.

Consider how the team influences people outside of the team.

Facilitated discussion: Trainer to set up the activity using template: Personal application planning

Ask: What styles are used most?

Influencing Strategies

Strategy	Stage	Key Tasks	Styles
Soft	State your view of problem	Concise presentation	PERSUADING
		Seeking feedback	INVOLVING
	Clarify other's perception	Listening	INVOLVING
	Agree problem (its existence)		
	Seek solutions		
	• Propose your own	Reflecting/summarising	INVOLVING
	• Invite their ideas	Questioning	INVOLVING
	• Joint best solution	Giving feedback	INSPIRING
Hard	Make proposal	Assertive presentation	ASSERTING
	Get reactions	Listening/summarising	PERSUADING
	Summarise and check	Questioning	INVOLVING
	Deal with objections	Generate commitment /Get compliance	INVOLVING ASSERTING
	Result	Summarise	INVOLVING

Deliverable:

A personal action plan to monitor influencing within the team.

Reflect on your influencing style, can you adopt other styles?

15: Influence Skills Exercise – Practice

Purpose: Apply basic influencing techniques and a range of communication techniques to support effective teamwork. Undertake a personal inventory check of the level of competence with influencing skills.

Instructions:

Understand the skills used in influencing. This session is divided into two segments and the second segment builds on the first segment.

In the first segment the trainer runs a short session to gather the skills they would use during a meeting when they are trying to influence another person. Participants can record the skills on workbook page: influencing skills notepad.

In the second segment the participants will work in trios to use the skills, and practice using the push and pull styles. Participants will be encouraged to give each other feedback on the use of the styles.

The trainer will work as a coach during the session, and then run a facilitated session to consider the process used within the influencing sessions.

Part 1: Understanding the skills used in influencing: team exercise to develop a list of skills to use while influencing, with review and agreement on the prime skills required.

Brief the team:

Two teams – each team uses post it notes to gather ideas. Then compares and contrasts to decide the key skills needed to influence.

Skills Used in Influencing – Giving Information to emphasize the two processes.

Part 2: Practice

Develop a relevant case study scenario to practice using the influencing skills and the different influencing styles with feedback.

Participants will be encouraged to use the influencing style, that they would not usually use and might prove to be challenging for them. They will be requested not to use their preferred style.

Brief participants:

Working in trios using the influencing scenarios

Each person will take a turn at:

- Observer: person who watches and gives feedback to the influencer;
- Influencer: Person who is practicing the skills;
- Target: person who is being influenced and is using the details in the scenario to help the influencer practice.

Each person will have 20 minutes air time when they are the influencer. Within the time they select the predefined scenario and has three minutes to prepare. They then test their skills using their selected style, and receive constructive feedback from the observer: what did they do well and a tip for improvement.

Reflection Time

At the end of the practice there will be personal reflection time to   consider which skills need improving and which styles to practice.

Deliverable:

Personal take of the level of competence with the skills.

Timing – 4 hours have elapsed – appropriate time for lunch

16: Conflict Handling – Theory and Mediated Practice

Purpose: Understand and agree on techniques to manage conflict. Apply a range of communication techniques to support effective teamwork.

Reference:

Pre-workshop task five: Read documentation provided that will contain background reading for the modules on Influencing and Conflict Handling.

Instructions:

The tools and techniques to manage conflict – based also on the influencing module. Workbook page: Understanding conflict – background information only.

Trainer can discuss the skills for the push and pull styles but only if there is sufficient time.

Trainer to explain, relating to Jean Lebedun model, that conflict is about differences and there are always varying points of view. We explore processes that assist with planning and resolving issues within the workplace.

The two models:

- Bridge the gaps in agreement by assessing the levels of conflict;
- Assess the situation by understanding different perceptions.

Emphasize the use of templates and processes, as an integral part of working as a high performing team and the effective use of time within the team.

Deliverable: Learn to use two conflict handling approaches.

1 - Four Levels of conflict

Discuss the levels of conflict and then brief the participants to take their "real life" scenarios to use in the exercise.

- Level 1: Conflict over facts and data;
- Level 2: Conflicts over process or methods;
- Level 3: Conflict over purpose;
- Level 4: Conflict over values.

Participants consider which level of conflict is embedded within the scenario and why the particular level of conflict has become an issue. In pairs or trios, the participants consider each other's scenario, and review the levels of conflict against each other's scenario. They then agree which level of conflict is appropriate for each scenario.

Participants to use: Workbook page; Levels of conflict

Assessing individual real life scenarios against the four levels of conflict, the pairs discuss the four levels and match to their scenario.

2 - Bridging the gaps in agreement

Assessing the situation by understanding different perceptions.

Discuss Robert Dilts perceptual positions, and brief the participants to consider their scenarios and list their thoughts from each of the three viewpoints.

See below:

- How do I define the situation – what are my facts, thoughts and ideas relating to the situation;
- How do others define the issue – especially the target, the person I have the issue with, define

the facts, what thoughts might they have on the issue, what ideas might they have relating to the situation;

- How would an observer define the issue – after hearing my point of view and the targets point of view, what thoughts might they have on the issue, what ideas might they have relating to the situation as an impartial observer

Discuss and debrief.

Participants to use workbook page: Influencing planning model.

Bridging the gaps to consider different perceptions using individual real life scenarios with review.

In pairs or trios review each scenario and add thoughts and ideas to build a multi description from the three viewpoints.

Deliverable:

Description of three perspectives.

Trainer material – Understanding Conflict

*"Conflict is a struggle between two parties who
perceive their goals as incompatible"*

The first part of the definition reminds us that
conflict always has two sides. They may be two
individuals or two groups of people. At work we
often see conflicts involving two shifts, two
departments, two regional divisions, or just two
factions that have drawn a battle around a particular
issue.

In managing conflict, your job is to find ways
that those goals can become compatible, so that both
sides can achieve part, most, or all of what they want.
It's a challenge, and it definitely requires a
partnership, not a war. Carefully analyzing the
conflict situation will help you begin to build that
partnership. Analyzing the emotions behind the
conflict and allowing those emotions to be expressed
are important first steps in conflict management.

Conflict happens

People at work have plenty to disagree about:
There is not enough material. There is not enough
time. There is not enough money. There are not

enough people. There is not enough space.

There are different ways of looking at things. There are different cultures. There are different needs. There are different plans. There are different views of ourselves, of the world, and where we fit into it all.

Conflict is about differences. People have different preferences, habits, and opinions, and sometimes those differences create conflict. Because of the expanding diversity of the workforce, we're seeing more conflict in the workplace than ever before.

Change also creates conflict in the workplace. During times of change, we experience high stress, unclear lines of responsibility, and lack of communication. All of these realities set up an ideal environment for conflict.

Reference: Managing Workplace Conflict – Jean Lebedun, Ph. D.

17: Conflict – Exercise

Purpose: To experiment with the conflict handling planning templates.

Pre-workshop task six: Select a real life scenario that involves influencing / handling conflict to use in a practice session.

Instructions:

Individual exercise; consider how to approach real life scenario in a practice session. Trainer to watch, advise, coach and give appropriate feedback.

Briefly outline the template; think it through, prepare and select your ground, take action to say what you would like to happen.

Tips for preparation:

- Which style to use: Push or Pull;
- Which level of conflict are is the participant dealing with;
- What information has the participant gleaned from the perceptual positions exercise;
- How much gathering of information will be done – asking questions;

- How much giving of information needs to be done.

Practice Session – the pairs are to practice a role play

Handling differences and conflict – Participants to work in pairs / trios to practice the skills handling differences and conflict.

Participants use "Real Life" situations to practice the skills and receive feedback relating to what worked well and tips for improvement.

In pairs - take it in turns to be the influencer and the target for the influencing scenario.

After each influencing practice stop and review: What went well? And what could be changed or done differently? The person who was the target should lead the feedback.

Then swap roles and repeat the exercise. Trainer to set timings.

Ensure all participants get a chance to practice.

Trainer to watch, advise, coach and give appropriate feedback.

Deliverable: Practice the skills of conflict handling and personal stock take on how well the team uses the skills.

18: Making It Happen – Interactive Concluding Exercise

Purpose: To consolidate of all the new team processes and skills.

Instructions:

Facilitated activity.

Picturing the journey the team needs to make:

- Our past – the old approach;
- Moving to Our Future – the new approach.

Collage Activity

Working in small teams, participants prepare a collage from newspapers and magazines depicting the old approach, and the move to the new approach and high performance.

The teams will also prepare a report back to the trainer and the other teams.

Review of their findings – trainer to facilitate a short discussion based on the output from the activity

Trainer to hold a facilitated discussion with the whole team regarding the learning from the exercise

Deliverable:

Consolidation of all the new team processes and skills.

19: Commitment

Purpose: Actions and commitments to adopt "Best Practice".

Instructions:

Action Planning

Trainer to brief the team on the activities using workbook page: Where do we go from here.

Use the slide: Team Process Review, to help focus the team and individuals on what they need to start and stop doing to move to a high performing team.

The output from the collage activity: our future – the new approach, is a good starting place and can act as the foundation for the team action plan.

Individuals prepare action plans

Individuals make commitments to help the process of team development.

The team agreed an action plan the first steps the team will take to develop their high performance team.

The trainer facilitates the activity and leads a learning review discussion to explore the action plans.

Deliverable:

Team and individual action plans

Post workshop activities

- Remind the participants that after the workshop the team and individuals should hold progress reviews;
- Individuals meet with their manager to discuss progress on their action plan;
- The team meets to consider how they are progressing with the team action plan.
- Team will use template used during the workshop.

Thank the individuals and the team

Close the workshop

Timing – End of second day

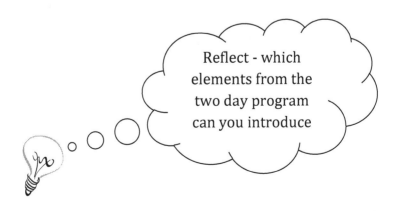

Reflect - which elements from the two day program can you introduce

Summary

Creating a high performance virtual team carries special challenges that don't exist for a collocated team. Most of these challenges emerge from the diversity of cultural backgrounds and the difficulty of communication. It is essential that the team develop communication protocols that allow for effective formal communication and informal communication.

The Internet provides numerous tools that can be used to develop these communication protocols. Actively using the available technology makes it possible to make isolated team members feel like integral parts of the team. As they feel more connected, they become more effective. As the **team members get to know each other better, they communicate and collaborate more, and the synergy of the team increases**.

Systems may have to be modified to work for the virtual team, especially systems that have been developed for static or collocated teams. Simple things that only take a few minutes to complete when everyone can meet physically become challenging when team members are scattered. Standards and policies might need to be modified to meet the team's needs.

The team leader is crucial to turning a team into a high performance team. He or she establishes the tone for the team. If he or she is positive, upbeat, goal oriented, and focused on helping the team members, the team will notice it and reflect those attitudes.

The more that the team leader is able to gain the confidence of the team, the better a chance they have of building that high performance team. Gaining team confidence comes from being honest, being concerned about them, doing what they say that they are going to do, and showing a genuine concern for the team member's needs.

Summary
of the
Must-Haves

Must-Have #1:
Develop Clear Goals and Plans

For any team to be effective, it needs to know where it is going and how it is going to get there. Goals and plans aren't merely dictated to the team from above, but developed by the team as a whole, including intermediate goals to be used as milestones.

While all plans suffer problems that cause them to be changed, without a plan, there is no way of knowing whether one is on track. However, it's not enough that the team develops clear goals. For the team to be high performance, every team member must buy into those goals as well. "Buy-in" is the surrendering of oneself for the greater good of the team's success. It has to be preached from the top-down and the behavior has to be modeled from top-down.

I have learned during my coaching practice that "buy-in" must be communicated in many forms, from motivational handouts to public praise for desired behavior. It is important that the communication occurs when appropriate.

"Buy-in" always occurs when the leader empowers the team members to create a culture in which the members are a part of the process. In this context, "buy-in" is more than inspirational quotes; it is a mentality, a belief; it is the core fabric that allows great things to happen collectively. Through the process of buying in, the team owns the goals and plans that they developed.

Must-Have #2:
Effective Communication

A team that doesn't communicate isn't a team at all, but a group of individuals who are each marching to the beat of their own drum. High performance teams develop clear, consistent methods for communicating with one another, both on a formal and informal basis. **This communication is both collaborative in nature and provides constant feedback to each team member**. By providing constant feedback, each team member feels more secure about the team relationship.

Must-Have #3:
Improve and Maintain Positive
Relationships between Members

For team members to work together effectively, their relationship needs to go beyond that of merely a business relationship. Members of high performance teams have social interactions outside the workplace, forming bonds between individual members based on respect, trust, and knowing one another's capabilities.

Time must be taken to develop and maintain these relationships; **this isn't wasted time, it is team-building time**.

Must-Have #4:
Clarify Roles and Responsibilities

The RACI model is a powerful tool utilized to define roles and responsibilities. In general, **you match up roles and responsibilities with processes.** RACI stands for

Responsible: The buck stops here. Whoever is responsible must make sure that the process operates as planned. The **R** owns the process, problem, or project.

Accountable: This is the person who is delegated the task of completing the activity. This person supports the person who owns the **R**.

Consult: This person usually has in-depth knowledge of the process in question and must approve all major decisions.

Inform: The people in this group need to be informed of activity taken, but not necessarily consulted in decisions made.

Must-Have #5:
Enhance Mutual Trust

Trust is one of the hardest qualities to develop in any team because it only happens through time and experience. Nevertheless, members of high performance teams must develop trust in each other and in the team overall.

Team members must see **competence and commitment** demonstrated by each other for this **trust** to grow. They must see that the other team members are committed to team success and not just to personal success. They need to develop confidence in each other both in professional and **personal integrity**.

Must-Have #6:
Solve Problems and Make Effective Decisions

In essence, teams make decisions using problem-solving techniques. Thus, the process largely rests on the selection of a **course of action following the evaluation of two or more alternatives.** To effectively navigate this path, a step-by-step approach can be used.

Must-Have #7:
Value and Promote Diversity

Often, the differences among individuals make them effective in what they do. Each one is able to bring his or her viewpoint and abilities to the table, adding something that nobody else on the team can add.

While small-minded people struggle with accepting those who are different, high performance teams accept and embrace the diversity of their members. They count on that diversity to provide the ideas necessary to create innovative solutions to problems. This can only happen when each team member is **willing to accept the others for who they are,** not belittling them for what they aren't.

Most global teams are aware of cross-cultural diversity, and organizations are investing in training and coaching of the various aspects of cultural diversity. Another type of diversity that is ever more apparent in contemporary teams and, when overlooked, **impedes the effectiveness** of the team is **cross-generation diversity**.

Must-Have #8:
Successfully Manage Conflict

In many cases, conflict in the workplace just seems to be a fact of life. We've all seen situations where different people with different goals and needs have come into conflict. And we've all seen the often-intense personal animosity that can result. **The fact that conflict exists, however, is not necessarily a bad thing.** As long as it is resolved effectively, conflict can lead to personal and professional growth. Effective conflict resolution can make the difference between positive and negative outcomes.

Must-Have #9:
Provide Development Opportunities and Recognition

While the team as a whole has goals for success, it recognizes that **each team member needs opportunities to succeed** in their own life and career. By helping team members find the opportunities to increase their individual skills and knowledge, they increase the ability of the overall team, increasing the team's probability for success.

Whether through a formal 360-degree instrument or informal conversations, it is important to give feedback on areas of strength or **developmental opportunities for all team members** and provide the training needed to enhance performance. Team member require some level of coaching support to attain new skills and reinforce new behaviors.

———

We covered the main methods, tools, and techniques to create and lead a virtual high performance team. Following these guidelines will enable you to lead your team to success. I'll be happy to answer your questions. Feel free to contact me.

sapir@sapir-cs.com

Thank you for your time, I hope you found this guide useful.

About the Author

Michael Nir, Transformation Inspiration Expert, Lean Agile Coach; empowers organizations to deliver results;

With over sixteen years of experience Michael has been leading change at global organizations in diverse industries. Committed to sustained results as well as the journey, Michael balances a passion for creativity and innovation alongside tested proven approaches for solution delivery. Michael inspires people and teams to change, cognitively and emotionally, building on enthusiasm from climbing the hill AND reaching the top.

In his toolbox are: agile product development and Scrum, project management know how, Lean Startup and Lean Agile expertise, change leadership and team building experience, and pragmatically integrating theory into practice.

Combining a BSc in Civil and MSc in Industrial Engineering from the prestigious Technion Institute of Technology, Michael aggregates technical acumen with study and practice of Gestalt therapy and Instrumental Enrichment, a philosophy of mediated learning. His clients represent a multitude of industries: Hi-tech, Banking, IT, Software, Health, Petrochemical and Infrastructure.

Sharing his knowledge and experience, Michael authored 10 bestsellers on Influencing, Lean Agile, Teams, and Leadership. The books engage readers in learning and motivate personal transformation.

PMP®, ACP®, SAFe® Program Consultant

Give the Gift of

Building Highly Effective Teams

to Your Friends and Colleagues

(Tear this page out, fill it in, scan and email it or mail it to the address at the bottom)

- ☐ I want to order _____ copies of the Agile PMO at $20 each, plus 3$ shipping per book. Orders of 24 or more books please call for volume discount. Canadian orders must be accompanied by a postal money order or check in U.S. funds or call us with credit card information. Allow 10 days for deliver.
- ☐ My check or money order for $_____ is enclosed.
- ☐ Please charge my Visa / Mastercard / Amex

Name: _____

Organization: _____

Address: _____

City/State/Zip: _____

Phone: _____ E-mail: _____

Card Number: _____

Exp. Date_____ Signature: _____

PLEASE MAKE YOUR CHECK PAYABLE TO SAPIR CONSULTINGAND
RETURN TO: 206 Gerry Rd, Chestnut Hill, MA 02467

Call your credit card order to 617-991-4253

E-mail us at: sapir@sapir-cs.com